How to Know If Your Prophecy Is Really From God

—And What to Do If It Is

Scott Wallis

Xulon Press
344 Maple Ave. West, #302
Vienna, VA 22180
703-691-7595
XulonPress.com

Dedication

I am so thankful for all the people who have brought God's prophetic word into my life. I have received wonderful prophecies that have encouraged and helped shape me into the man that I am today. For this I am grateful.

I have also been blessed with some extraordinary relationships. God has given me good people who have stood by me through thick and thin. Ron, I appreciate the blessing you have been throughout the years. Your friendship means alot. Thank you.

Mom, you are one in a million. God gave me the best, when He gave me to you. You have been a faithful Mom, always loving, and always kind. Your generousity to me has spurred me to give more than I take, and do more than has been done for me.

Most of all, this book is dedicated to my Lord and Savior, Jesus Christ, who became my friend while I was still a sinner. You took me into your heart, loved me and gave me a reason for living. I am forever grateful for who you have made me to be. I love you.

Contents

Foreword

Dear Reader,

You are about to read a great book. If you allow it to, it can change your life. It will teach you more than just how to evaluate and act on prophetic words; it will teach you about the essence of prophecy—submitting your life to God's will.

Submitting to God's will has not always been easy for me. I have had many thoughts regarding God's will for my life that were not true. I have learned, as you are about to, that God truly does have the best plans for our lives—He wants the best for us. God wants us to be happy and fulfilled in this life. Something that I have not always believed.

I first met Scott Wallis in 1992, at a men's retreat. We just happened to bump into each other in the hallway one day and started talking. Scott began sharing with me how he was in the process of completing a book filled with prophecies regarding the future and destiny of America.

As "chance" would have it, this was a topic of real interest to me. I wanted to hear more about what he was saying regarding prophecy, but things were so hectic in the meeting that I didn't have a chance to get his number. Thankfully, I remembered him telling me where he went to church so I called his pastor.

It is somewhat hard for me to describe where I was at in my life at this time. I would never have admitted to myself or anyone else that I was living a common American life—one filled with quiet desperation. I had no peace or passion. I loved the churches that I had been to, but oftentimes I wondered if there was more. My job met my basic needs, but would never allow me to fulfill my dreams. I was comfortable materially, but not satisfied with my position in life. My wife and I love each other, but we both wanted more.

I didn't know it at the time, but God wanted to bless me in these areas and more. He wanted to give me more than what I wanted, or would even dare ask Him at the time. God had better plans for me than I had for myself. I could never have imagined where God would take me, or even believe that He would bring me to where I am at today.

My life has changed dramatically these past eight years. It is almost hard for me to believe where I am at today. I am a changed man, one who is living the American dream. My perception of God has changed. I can honestly say that I know God is for me. My perception of myself has changed. I now enjoy my own company. And if someone else doesn't like me, or something I do, I can handle it. I haven't always been way.

My home has God's peace. My relationship with my wife, Julie, is so good, warm, loving and fulfilling that it is hard to believe we have only just begun to enter into what God has for us. I have three wonderful little girls: Hannah, Sarah and Rachel who love God and their Sunday school teacher (me). We enjoy our church, one that we helped plant about a year ago. God has truly prospered us.

What does any this have to do with Scott Wallis? He is the man that God has used to communicate His blessing into my life. Scott has been a faithful prophetic voice to me and my family. Through him, I have learned how to know God's will and ways, and quite frankly, it is better than I could have asked or hoped possible.

How did this happen? Much of it happened the way that Scott talks about in this book—step by step. I have been blessed, covered, guided, taught and occasionally corrected by Scott's prophetic ministry. God has used him tremendously in my life to help me understand and walk this fantastic journey called life.

God longs to do the same things for you that He has done for me. God hasn't done what He's done for me because I am special, or because I have spent more time seeking Him than you. Why, then, has He done these things for me? He has done these things for me because I have been willing to do things His way. I have been willing to listen to His voice and do what He has asked me to do. Not that I have always been as obedient as I would like to be. There are still things in my life that I struggle with at times. But I am making great strides in living for Him. And, we all know God saves the best wine for last.

This is what knowing Scott Wallis has done in my life. He has been a true prophet to me and my family. He is a man of great faith, tremendous moral character, goodness and love. He has taught me how to hear and obey God. A process, by the way, that is not always as ethereal, smooth or easy as we would like. Sometimes it has been visceral, gritty and hard, but it has never been more than I could handle with God's grace. And, it has born so much good fruit in my life that I cannot completely convey this to you.

My hope and prayer is that this book will be as much a blessing to you as knowing Scott has been to me. I believe that God will greatly bless you through this book and that you will learn how to hear from Him through His spokesman—His prophets. And it is as you learn how to do this that you will receive all that He has for you.

Sincerely,
Ron Eriksen

Introduction

Prophecy is one of the most misunderstood subjects in the body of Christ today. Over the past decade, prophetic ministry has come to the forefront of the mind of the church. We have learned that God truly does want to speak to us today. This understanding has caused us to elevate prophecy to a higher place in the church. We have started to see that prophecy can be a blessing to us, and as a result, many want to receive prophetic ministry.

This is good, but along with the good of prophecy has come the bad, and in some cases the ugly. Many involved in prophetic ministry can be downright flaky. In some cases, common sense is completely absent. Ministers can use prophecy to gain control over the minds of their followers and cause them to do some really stupid things. We have come to view the bizarre as normal in the church. What is wrong with this picture?

Honoring God's Prophets

In the Old Testament, prophets were among the most respectable people. God trained His prophets in holiness before He used them as spokesmen. God spoke to His prophets, and as a result, their words were filled with the spirit of conviction. The prophetic word was a source of conviction and revelation. Many left their sinful ways and returned to God because of it. Through their lives, prophets made prophecy respectable.

In the Old Testament, the prophet was a respectable profession. Many would flock to prophets to hear from God concerning their lives. They knew that God was in their midst, and that there was nothing wrong with seeking Him for specific answers to their questions. People would often come to prophets bearing gifts. They did this with the expectation of hearing from God. This was one of the unwritten requirements of hearing from God through prophets (1 Sam. 9:6-8).

Samuel lived by this system, and so did Elijah. Some of God's greatest prophets recognized that it was important for people to bless them before receiving the prophetic word. They knew that unless the people believed in what they were saying, the prophetic word would be useless to them. Even if the prophetic word did come to pass, if the people had not received it in faith, it would not benefit them. The Jewish people supported the prophet, and as a result were blessed by God's prophetic ministry.

Today, if someone tried to live this way, he would most likely be accused of being a false prophet. People might call him a Balaam or charlatan or some other name, but it certainly would not be good. Somehow, the church culture has come to view this type of support for prophets as being evil when, in reality, God is the one who instituted it. Jesus made this statement about providing for prophets: "He that receiveth a prophet in the name of a prophet shall receive a prophet's reward" (Matt. 10:41).

God—not man—has created this system of support for prophets. I want you to understand something: Prophets have bills to pay and families to feed just like you. Prophets are people who need to receive wages for the work they perform (1 Tim. 5:18). In their case, the work they do is the words they give.

The question is: How do we place a value on genuine prophecy?

Prophets and Prophecy in the Church

Even now, you may be asking yourself the question: Does this mean that we can buy prophetic words? The obvious answer to this question is no. Prophetic words cannot be bought, sold, or transferred like stocks, bonds, or options. We cannot buy a prophetic word, but I do believe that as we bless prophets, their prophetic words will bless us. Also, the blessing that comes upon us through the prophetic word can be rescinded through a lack of support for prophets.

I have said this because much of the church has very little understanding of their relationship with prophets. As a result, many of the prophetic words that have been given have failed to come to pass. The church is filled with unrealized prophetic promise because we have had some wrong impressions regarding prophets and prophecy.

I want to discuss some of those wrong impressions in this book. I believe it is important for us to receive a Biblical understanding of prophets and prophecy if we want to receive their blessings. This book is not an end-all, be-all book, and it is not meant to repeat what other authors have written regarding prophets

and prophecy. I have written this book to meet a per-
ceived need in the body of Christ that has not been
discussed, namely, "How to know if your prophecy is
really from God—and what to do if it is."

This subject in some ways is like handling a hot
potato. Everyone perceives a problem, but few have
wanted to tackle this issue of unfulfilled prophecy, or
have understood how to go about it. The reasons for
this are many. In some cases it is ego, in others fear.
No one wants to hear that they are responsible for the
fulfillment of a prophetic word. It is easier to believe
that if something is God's will, it will come to pass.
After all, every genuine prophecy must come to pass.
Right?

Wrong! Prophecy doesn't just come to pass; it must
be fulfilled. What do I mean by this? I mean that
what we do, or don't do, will have a direct impact
upon the fulfillment of the prophecies we receive
(Heb. 4:2). Does this mean that we can receive a genuine prophecy and still not have it come to pass? Yes!
You may receive one from the most accurate prophet
in the world today, but not have it be fulfilled because
you have not taken the steps necessary for that word
to come to pass in your life.

This is why it is important for us to know what
God expects us to do when we receive a prophecy. A

series of steps must be taken for every prophetic word received. These steps are designed to help you see the fulfillment of those God-anointed and -appointed words you receive, and avoid the pitfalls of false or inaccurate prophecy.

Our Responsibility in Receiving Prophecy

God wants you to have what He has promised you through prophecy. It is God's way of communicating the riches that He has prepared for us in Christ. Therefore, knowing how prophecy comes to pass, and the things we can do to help in its fulfillment, are very important to our destiny as believers. It is your right to share in the privilege of receiving prophecy, and your responsibility to see it fulfilled in your life.

God did not design His work to be viewed through the eyes of a spectator. We are active participants in God's plans, including those plans revealed through the vehicle of prophecy. This means that for prophecy to be fulfilled in our lives, it must be done. Now there are certain parts that are your responsibility, and certain parts that are God's responsibility. If we do what we are supposed to do, we can trust Him to do what He promises to do.

Prophecy is always conditional upon our response to it (1 Cor. 13:8). This means that how we receive, react, and respond to prophecy will, in some ways, have a direct impact upon its fulfillment in our lives. You have a part to play in the fulfillment of God's will in your life. Your future is shaped and affected by what you do, or don't do, in line with God's will. Prophecy is a glimpse into God's mind. He wants to help us understand how to align our lives with His will.

God's grace and mercy are the attributes that cause Him to speak to us prophetically. He doesn't want us to wander aimlessly through this life without knowing His will. He has invested a great deal in all of us. We are important to Him. He longs to communicate with us through prophecy so that we can have purposeful and meaningful lives.

What we do in this life is extremely important to God (Col. 3:23,24). This is why God will often speak to us through prophecy about several areas of our lives. Sometimes prophecy will encourage, while other times it will comfort us over a loss. It may be filled with tough love, or it may be overflowing with His grace. Prophecy can direct, correct, comfort, encourage, exhort, reveal, impart, activate, or bless us.

Why Prophecy Is a Good Gift

Prophecy is one of God's greatest gifts to us, for it

can enable us to do what we never dreamed possible. It enables us to peer into the realm of the impossible and see it become reality. This is why prophecy and miracles often work hand in hand. For you to receive the fulfillment of a prophecy, often a miracle will need to take place. You will also need to have faith that God can do what He promised.

Prophecy is designed to spark our faith in the God we serve. It will increase our faith, expand our vision, and create an atmosphere for the supernatural. It has the power to move us beyond where we are right now, causing us to believe, receive, and achieve more for God's kingdom than we ever thought possible. Prophecy is the language God uses to communicate His faith into our hearts.

This is why prophecy is so valuable. Faith is the gift of God and cannot be manufactured by man. We cannot force ourselves to believe God for the impossible. God desires to create faith in our hearts so we will believe Him, even for what is beyond our own reason. God gains glory for Himself through the faith demonstrated in our lives. It should be our desire for God to receive glory from our lives through fulfilled prophecy. The ultimate goal of this book is to help you bring glory to God.

Prophecy brings glory to God when it is fulfilled,

and it also imparts the glory of God to our lives. This is one way we can tap into the glory of God. I believe that every prophecy fulfilled in our lives releases a corresponding measure of God's glory.

Prophecy is a blessing when understood in the light of scripture. When we understand God's goal for giving us a prophetic word, and what our responsibility is upon receiving it, we will be ready to receive the associated blessing. When we look in scripture, God's blessing and prophecy are almost synonymous—one does not exist without the other.

Consequently, false or inaccurate prophecy can be devastating to those who receive it. It can strangle the blessing that God desires to pour out through genuine prophecy. All prophecy must be judged. According to scripture, "Let the prophets speak two or three, and let the other judge. If anything be revealed to another that sitteth by, let first hold his peace" (1 Cor. 14:29,30).

Handling Prophecy Wisely

God, through Paul, instituted instructions at Corinth to protect it from false or inaccurate prophecies. God has called prophets to govern prophecy in the church. When prophecy is correctly governed in the church, the church has a greater level of protection from false or inaccurate prophecy.

We must realize that God has not called one man to do everything in the church. Most pastors know that they do not have the tools necessary to deal with prophecy. A pastor with no prophetic gifting trying to govern prophecy in the church is like a car mechanic trying to perform surgery. He would soon realize that he is in over his head, uncertain of what to do, and appearing to have a giant question mark on his face. If that's you, stop it. Use the gift and calling that God gave you.

Even among prophets, there are different levels of administration and authority. Some prophets have local ministries, and minister to local churches. Others will travel to many cities, regions, or even nations. Some will be effective in personal prophecy. Others will be more effective in prophesying to churches and ministries. Some will speak to those in business, and others to those in politics. We cannot use the same rule and expect everyone to conform to it.

God has not made all prophets the same, and neither has He given to every prophet the same level of authority or influence in the body of Christ. An important way that prophetic authority is established is through the favor that God gives to His prophets.

If I have favor with one group of people, it does not necessarily mean that I have favor with everyone. Prophets must realize that favor among the people to whom they minister is a sign of the authority that they have with that particular group.

God will hold prophets accountable for the words they speak through several different means. One is through other prophets with equal or greater authority. Another is through those to whom they minister the prophetic word. If a prophet ministers in a church, there is nothing wrong with the pastor holding that prophet accountable for the words they have ministered. Ultimately, God will hold His prophets accountable through the favor that He gives to them (1 Cor. 4:3-5).

A Healthy Perspective of Prophets

Why is it so important for us to understand these things? There are a couple of reasons, one of which is that God does not take it lightly when we judge prophets. We may judge prophecy, but we must be careful in judging prophets. Prophets, like pastors, are God's representatives on earth—we need to respect them and give them the honor that is due them (Rom. 13:7). They are fully functioning members of the fivefold ministry, and have been given authority by God to minister to His people (Eph. 4:11-13).

Most people would never think of carelessly accusing their pastors of giving wrong counsel or calling them hirelings if they asked people to pay their tithes. God has given pastors these responsibilities. When a pastor gives counsel or accepts tithes, he is fulfilling the mandate of scripture. Anyone who falsely accuses a pastor of wrongdoing when he is obeying God would most likely be censured by the church, and rightly so.

In the same way, God has anointed prophets for their role in the church. Prophets have authority from God to fulfill the will of God and to bring the word of the Lord. This is part of their function as ministers. When they receive money for doing this, they are doing what God says is good, just, and right in His word. Who are we to condemn them? Who are we to lightly judge them? Why do we think that God will approve if we judge, accuse, or slander them falsely?

We must fear God and depart from evil (1 Pet. 2:17, 1 Pet. 3:11). It is time for the church to receive wisdom regarding prophetic ministry. For years, I have seen many people who think nothing of bad-mouthing, accusing, or slandering other ministers. Who do we think we are? Will not God deal with us in our bad attitude? Could this be a reason why our prophecies have failed us, or rather we have failed them?

We Desperately Need Good Prophecy

It is time for the church to grow up. Leaving behind the fallacies that we so doggedly cling to, we must return to the Bible and rediscover what it has to say. We must stop behaving as modern-day Pharisees and become genuine disciples of Christ. Our lives—not our eloquence—determine the credibility of what we say.

Paul said, "I came to you, not with wise and persuasive words of man's wisdom, but in demonstration of the Spirit and power, that your faith should not stand on the wisdom of men but the power of God" (1 Cor. 2:1,4). We desperately need prophetic ministry to be restored in our day. It opens the door to God's work in our lives. As Amos says, "Surely the Lord God will do nothing but He revealeth His secrets unto His servants the prophets" (Amos 3:7). If God has this kind of respect for prophets and prophetic ministry, should we have any less?

I want to encourage you to read through this book carefully and thoroughly. It is a guide to help you see the fulfillment of the prophetic words you have received. If you follow the principles spoken of in this book, you will not only see your prophecies fulfilled, but your destiny as well. May God use this book to help you fulfill His will in your life.

Chapter One

Prophecy 101

A s you have probably concluded from the introduction, I am in favor of prophecy and
prophets. In fact, I am a prophet myself. God called
me to be His prophet from birth, even though I was-
n't saved or Spirit-filled until 1987. I did not even
know that Jesus died for my sins until I was 22 years
old. This was my first encounter with God, and it
resulted in my salvation. Little did I know that God
had His hand upon me from birth, even using a
Catholic priest to prophesy about my calling to my
mother and grandmother.

Even though I personally don't remember it, this was when I was first introduced to prophecy. It has always played an important role in my relationship with God. Without it, I truly don't know where I would be today. Prophecy has done more for me than I can convey to you within the pages of this book. I have been healed, delivered, and guided by it. Where I am today in my walk with God is because of prophecy.

What I have learned hasn't come just through books, but rather through experiencing God working in my life through prophecy. It is for this reason that I want you to read what is in this chapter about it. This is an introduction to the subject; it is designed to help you better understand the purpose of prophecy and what it should do in our lives.

The Prophetic Mantle

Prophecy is a gift from God to the church. The church desperately needs this gift today, especially with the advent of psychics, soothsayers, and fortune-tellers selling their services on many television stations. Millions of people are turning to the devil for guidance in their lives, and the church needs to rise up in response to this assault upon the hearts and minds of men and women. It is time for us to grow up and learn about this precious gift that Christ has deposited in us by His Holy Spirit.

The Bible, speaking to the believer, says, "For ye may all prophesy one by one, that all may learn, and all may be comforted" (1 Cor. 14:31). This means that it is God's will for you to prophesy. The spirit of prophecy rests upon you through the person of the Holy Spirit. You may or may not be a prophet, but you are qualified, anointed, and appointed by God to speak for Him. God has designed you to be an oracle to those around you where people can come to hear the Holy Spirit.

1 Peter 4:11 says, "If any speak, let him speak as the oracles of God..." It is our holy calling as Christians to speak for God to everyone around us, believers and unbelievers alike. The scripture even says that our simple testimony of Christ's work in our lives is the spirit of prophecy. We have been anointed to prophesy. You are prophetic, whether or not you think so, because the church itself is a prophetic organization.

The church has been given the mantle of prophecy. When the church speaks, the world should intently listen to what it is saying (Phil. 2:16). What happens in the church has a direct bearing on what happens in the world. When the church falters or fails to stand up and speak for God, the world slips ever deeper into evil. Where there is no light, darkness will prevail. When the church fails to bring forth truth, the world waits in vain for the holy light of prophecy to shine forth and call it out of darkness.

Christ has called you out of darkness for a purpose: to speak for Him to those around you. You are a light, and according to Jesus, a city that is set upon a hill cannot be hidden. God has put you on a pedestal to declare His word to those around you. The light that is in you cannot be hidden, for it is Christ in you, the hope of glory, who is shining through you. His light can never be snuffed out, and neither can His voice through the vehicle of prophecy.

As long as Christ is seated at the right hand of God, His voice will be heard through the prophetic word. God has chosen in these last days to speak to His church through the voice of His Son. We are His hands as well as His mouth, and unless we speak up, Christ will not be heard by the world. We must take the responsibility to be His voice to this generation. The question is, are we willing to take a stand and speak for Him, no matter what others may say to us?

Becoming a Prophetic Voice
to the World

You are an anointed servant of Christ. Prophecy is a mighty weapon in your arsenal against the forces of hell that are standing in your way and shaping our world today. We must allow God to loose this mighty sword through us, His church, so that we can win the battle against these sinister forces of darkness. We must not allow the powers of hell to claim a victory through our failure to stand for what is right by being a prophetic voice to those around us.

God has called His church to be a prophetic voice to the world. We are to prophesy, preach, and pray until the day Jesus comes again. Our goal must be to stand up and speak the truth in love, no matter what others may say about us (Eph. 4:15). Being a prophetic voice does not come easily; it can be extremely difficult to speak for the truth, especially when no one else wants to hear it. As a result, prophecy often comes with many casualties. To prophesy means to declare war against darkness.

This is why the devil hates prophecy. A church that speaks for God to the world is a threat to his kingdom. The devil will do anything he can to silence the voice of God by disabling the vehicle of prophecy. This is a reason why prophecy has been so hotly contested in the church. Prophets are easy targets for the devil, and he will use any means possible to stop them from declaring the word of God to the church and the world.

A Prophet's Footsteps

Being a prophet is not all that it is cracked up to be. Prophets often go through hell to hear from heaven. The visions and revelations they receive from God are fleeting, especially in the face of overwhelming obstacles, misunderstandings, and difficulties (James 5:10). Prophets are often treated poorly, especially by those who know them. When people do receive them, it usually isn't for very long. I have found through experience that people usually have a very low tolerance for prophets.

Many prophets have to keep on moving from city to city to increase their audience. Those who choose to live this way often see their ministries grow, but at the expense of their relationships. It is hard to maintain an attitude of accountability when one does not interact with the same people every week. This is why prophets are often lonely people. They know the price they must pay to hear from God, and few of those around them are willing to pay that price consistently.

I have found as a prophet that very few are willing to walk with me down the path that God has chosen for me. It isn't that people dislike the excitement associated with prophetic ministry; in fact, many do enjoy it. But the cheering lasts for a very short time. They soon discover that many grueling trials constitute much of the prophet's life. This is the dark side of prophetic ministry that few are aware of. As such, when confronted with these trials, most people will simply walk away rather than walk through them.

I believe this is why Jesus stated that those who receive a prophet will receive a prophet's reward. Those who support and bless the prophet are often blessed with spiritual well-being and financial wealth, as well as physical, mental, and relational health, all for the sake of His servants.

The Prophet's Reward

I am amazed at what God has done for those He has used to support me as a prophet. Most find their lives more fulfilling and rewarding. Those who have blessed me have in some cases become rich, by just being obedient in giving manageable amounts of support. When they have done what God told them to do, they were blessed. God even blessed those who didn't do all that He asked of them, as they were helping me as much as they were able.

How would you like this to happen in your life? It can! Find a prophet of God and bless him. God is no respector of persons in this regard. If you bless His prophets, you will be blessed by the Almighty God. God has promised this in His word for all who obey Him, and He cannot, yea will not, violate His word. When you support a prophet, you are making a quality investment that will pay immediate dividends toward the quality of your life. You will also receive eternal rewards and an ability to fulfill your destiny in Christ.

Prophets and prophecy are vital to the church. Every believer needs to hear from God through this divine vehicle. Since this is true, what is prophecy, and how can I tell if someone is a prophet? These are important questions that we must find the answers to in the word of God. The Bible has clear answers to these questions. Let us therefore see what the scriptures reveal about prophets and prophecy.

God Is Speaking Today

What is prophecy? Prophecy, in its simplest form, is God speaking to one person through another. God can speak to us at any time and any place if we have ears to hear what He is saying. This is why we must cultivate a heart that desires to hear from Him. Hearing God is foundational to our understanding of prophecy, for without a desire to hear God, we will miss most of what God is speaking to us.

Prophecy can take on many different forms. God usually uses individuals to speak to us prophetically, but not always. God will also often use natural events or life's circumstances. He can also use supernatural events such as dreams, visions, trances, angelic visitations, or visitations from the Lord Himself. All of these are prophecy, and God can use these at any time, in any place.

Why is God willing to take such measures to speak to us? Because unless we hear from Him, we are truly lost in this world. We cannot do God's will without His help, and part of that help is divine guidance. We need this spiritual compass of prophecy to keep us on track in the will of God and to safely navigate our way through the challenges of life. Without this spiritual compass, we will almost certainly run aground and become shipwrecked on the shores of life.

The Language of God

God doesn't want this to happen, so He has gone to great lengths to develop a language for us to hear

Him. Prophecy is the language of God to mankind; it is God communicating His mind and heart to us, using words we can understand, to convey what He is thinking about us (1 Cor. 2:10-12). Why does God have to communicate with us in this manner? Because it would be impossible for us to understand Him otherwise, for His thoughts are far above ours. Prophecy conveys what is on God's heart and mind.

God speaks to us through human words to convey His wisdom and understanding about our lives. Those who prophesy are therefore prophesying only in part. Every person prophesying is subject to limitations that prevent them from clearly communicating everything that God is saying. As these imperfections are removed, God's words can be more clearly heard and understood.

Many people have focused on removing these imperfections from God's prophets in hopes of hearing from God more clearly. And while I think that this is good, there is a danger in doing this: We begin to think of prophecy in human terms rather than with God's divine wisdom and understanding. When this happens, we reduce prophecy to our level rather than allowing prophecy to bring us to God's level, which it is designed to do.

Prophecy Is God Working on Us

Prophecy should challenge and change us. Every prophecy from God has power to be fulfilled if properly understood and applied (Eccl. 8:4). In scripture there is a greater emphasis on receiving, hearing, and applying prophecy than on instructing how to speak prophetically (Rev. 2:29). This is contrary to what is taught today, where most of the emphasis is placed on the one speaking prophetically.

This does not excuse those who mislead or do not give accurate prophecies. (I will talk more about false and inaccurate prophecies in the next chapter.) Accuracy is very important to the prophetic ministry; this is what we must strive for in the words that we give. However, a word being accurate does not mean that it is a good prophecy; neither does it ensure that the word spoken to us will come to pass in our lives.

Judging Prophecy

We therefore need to learn what makes good prophecy and what is required in the fulfillment of prophecy. The scripture says to prove all things and to hold fast to what is good, and to let every word be established in the mouths of two or three witnesses. These are good rules to follow when we receive prophecy. We should never hang our hats on a prophecy that is unproven or untested. We must test the words that are given to us, no matter who they come from.

Every prophecy must be judged. The scriptures declare, "Let the prophets speak two or at most three, and let the other judge. If anything be revealed to another that sitteth by, let the first hold his peace" (1 Cor. 14:29,30). Paul said, "these are the commandments of the Lord" (1 Cor. 14:37). In other words, these are not just good ideas, but God's ideas about prophecy. We should give heed to what the scriptures have to say to us. Following these simple steps would resolve many of the problems the church is struggling with about prophecy.

Pastors, Prophets and Prophecy

I have found that a major problem that many pastors have with prophecy is they just don't know how to handle it. This can be a real dilemma, especially if a pastor has a number of people who can prophesy in his congregation. This is why I want to encourage such pastors to step away from it unless they know that they are called to minister in this area. God has not given most pastors the gifts necessary to help prophets. It takes a mature prophet to assist other prophets.

I know what some of you pastors are thinking. You have been taught that God has called you to pastor the prophetic. This is a wrong teaching that is not founded on the precepts of scripture. What the scriptures say is that prophets are to judge prophecy. This means that we need to have a team concept of ministry. If prophecy is to function in the church, we need to allow prophets to govern it. Does this mean that we are to totally turn the service over to prophets? Hardly! But we must let them govern that part of the service to which they are called, and to give them time to do it.

When pastors let go of this area of ministry, it can be as liberating as having an accountant come in and help with taxes. None of us would think twice about hiring an accountant to help with the church books. In fact, it would be foolish to try and do an accountant's job if one is not trained in it, and could potentially lead to trouble. The same is true with prophecy. If you are not called to do it, stay out of it, and just nod your head a lot at the person you ask to lead it.

Genuine Prophecy Will Grow Your Church

I believe that a correct understanding of prophecy

produces many blessings in the lives of those who hear it. Prophecy is good for the church; it will help your church to grow. Nothing—and I do mean nothing—can draw a crowd to your church like someone who can speak for God. People will come from miles around just to be a part of it. The members of your congregation will be happier, healthier individuals. They will find their purpose and calling in Christ. They will prosper and be healthy, for their soul will prosper (3 John 2). This is what the Bible says.

Hearing from God is vital to the growth and survival of the church. A church that cannot hear God is one that will not obey God. We cannot obey the voice of God if we are not willing to hear from Him. We must therefore radically change our understanding of the nature of prophecy and prophets, allowing God to soften our hearts to this ministry. If we don't, we are placing ourselves on a dangerous precipice of self-destruction.

Rocking the Boat and Waking the Church

According to most church historians, the church left to its own devices tends to rot from within by straying away from God's call. As we move further and further away from our calling, we move into the rot of human opinion and understanding. This rot within the church creates a rut that few are able to escape. This is what Christ said to His disciples, "Let them alone: they be blind leaders of the blind. And if the blind lead the blind, both shall fall into the ditch" (Matt. 15:14).

How many ditches have we dug because of our unwillingness to hear the voice of God? Only heaven knows. More danger exists in a church that cannot hear from God than in one that hears Him through static. Although it is ideal that the static be removed from the prophecy we hear, we place ourselves in immense danger by not listening at all to prophecy or prophets.

The prophetic voice is therefore very important to the church. We need God to raise up prophets with clear voices, free from the static of human opinion. This does not happen overnight. Samuels are not as common as we would hope. Quite often because of sin, there is no open vision in the church (1 Sam. 3:1). We desperately need God to raise up genuine prophetic voices, with a calling to serve within the church.

The prophetic office should never be treated lightly. Neither should we make the mistake of mocking prophets, as the children did who mocked Elisha. They paid severely for their mistake and were mauled by bears. How many bears have mauled the church because we have mocked God's anointed prophets? I am not saying we should not call for accuracy in prophecy, but we should never mock the prophetic ministry or the prophetic word (1 Thess. 5:20).

Turning Up the Volume

Since the prophetic office is so important to the church, how does God raise up His prophets? Ideally, the church should be a place that cultivates the prophetic ministry so prophets would be raised up within it. However, this is not the case in most churches today. Few churches, if any, have places for budding prophets to develop their gifts. And even those that are receptive often fail to understand the true value of what they have—a conduit for God's voice.

The church, by and large, is not ready to receive prophets into its fold. Most pastors or Christian leaders find it easier to put prophecy on the back burner rather than to allow growth through active use of this gift of God. This has created unbelievable tension in prophets who are called to speak. It is as if we have put our hands over God's mouth. How many of you would dare do this? And yet this is often what we do in every service when we silence the budding prophetic voices in our midst.

No wonder God takes His prophets, especially those who are young, outside of the church to raise them up into full stature when we have not received them. Senior prophetic voices in the church are often guilty of this. Few have wanted the task of cleaning up a budding prophet's mistakes. There is little glory or glamour in this. As a result, prophetic fathers are often absent in the lives of their aspiring protégés. It is easier to allow the television ministries to raise our developing prophets than to do it ourselves.

This is why the prophetic ministry is in such disrepute among so many leaders. We have no one to blame but ourselves. We have tried to place our hands upon God's holy oracle, as Uzzah did, and we have paid dearly for it (2 Sam. 6:6,7). We need to repent, as David did for using a new ox cart to carry in the holy presence of God to Jerusalem. As we repent, God will open our hearts to hear how we can carry the holy ark of prophecy into the church once again.

Bringing Prophecy Back Into the Church

Let us not deceive ourselves into thinking everything is okay. It is not. We cannot continue to carry the ark of prophecy into the church as we have without severe consequences. As leaders in the prophetic, our repentance will prepare the hearts of leaders in the church to receive budding prophets into their midst. As a prophet, I am speaking to other senior prophetic leaders: we have a lot of foot-washing to do in the church (John 13:5,14).

Until we are ready to humble ourselves and to receive the ministry that God has given us to father the prophetic, we will never see the reproach of false or inaccurate prophecy removed from the church. And the longer that we allow this cancer to grow, the greater the danger of being cut off from the rest of the body (Matt. 5:29,30). The body is reacting to what it sees as a threat. We must allow God to graft us in His way so we can be received as members of the body.

By the way, the church longs for this to happen. Most of those within the church long to hear from God. The wonder and awe of hearing God is overwhelming. This is the joy that should fill the church. Yet for this to happen, we need to allow God to repair the bridges that have been destroyed through false or inaccurate prophecy. We must humble ourselves for God to exalt us to the position He wants us to hold in His body. But are we willing to do this?

God Is Cleaning His House

I am amazed by the pride in the prophetic ministries of our day. Few prophets have truly humbled themselves in the sight of God, let alone man. We have paid a dear price for our pride; it has alienated us from the body of Christ and leaders within the church. The church has not received prophetic ministry because they are afraid of it—and with good reason, I might add. The truth is that we have marketed a defective product that is a potential safety hazard to all who use it. This must change.

Not only must there be a change in prophetic ministry, especially in its leaders. The church itself and its leaders must change as well. Pride dwells in pastors at least as much as in prophets. Pastors, and in some cases new apostles, have sought to place prophets in a box. They attempt to control the prophetic voice in the church, forcing prophets to say what they want. Is this not sin? And will not God chastise us for it?

We must hear what the Spirit is saying to the church. The Spirit is calling for massive repentance from prophets and the church alike. The time for change has come. We must hear this clear voice from the Spirit of God. The prophetic cloud is moving, and the requirements for prophecy in the church are changing. God is cleaning up His house (1 Pet. 4:17).

He is calling for attitudes toward prophetic ministry to change among all believers.

The Clarion Call of Christ

God's clarion call will go forth from the prophetic office and bring the joyful sound of prophecy into the church once again. This is the new call of the prophetic ministry, and pastors and other leaders will be required by God to listen. Those who do will be blessed, and those who don't will not. It is that simple. Are you ready?

I know that what I am saying may be blunt. I intend to be this way to bring clarity to the truth about prophets and prophetic ministry. There must be a new holiness around the sound of "Thus Saith the Lord." We must separate the clean from the unclean. We must take the precious from the vile so that we, the church of the Lord Jesus Christ, can be the mouth God has called us to be to the world (Jer. 15:19).

I believe that one of the greatest needs within the church today is sound judgment and godly wisdom regarding prophecy. We need discernment. We need to know how to identify what is real and what is false. We cannot assume that just because someone says, "thus saith the Lord," that the Lord is speaking through them. We cannot be naïve in this area, or we may lose the virtue and value of genuine prophecy. Admittedly this is harder than it sounds, for it is easy to fall into the ditch on both sides of the way.

My hope and prayer is that we would receive the grace necessary to avoid this ditch of false and inaccurate prophecy. It is only as we do so that we will be able to move forward in understanding of why prophecies fail. And as much as I hate to admit it, this is one of the main reasons prophecies fail: they are not from God. The scriptures talk about this in depth, and we need to hear what they have to say on this matter of false and inaccurate prophecies. This is what I will present in the next chapter.

Chapter Two

Raising the Prophecy Standard

The church today needs a clarion call from the prophetic ministry. So many distractions surround us that it is hard to get a clear picture of the battle that we are fighting. The trumpets, God's prophetic voices, have been producing unclear sounds, and have been sending the wrong message to the church (1 Cor. 14:8). This wrong message is that prophets do not know what they are doing. This is not a good message to send, especially from leaders within the prophetic movement. Hence, it is time that we change our tune.

The church needs a clear message from the prophetic community. Accuracy in what we say is important, and so is clarity in our communication. Christ's character must be exalted and our own fleshly interests diminished (John 3:30). There can be no ulterior motives behind our words. Therefore, we must not sell our prophecies to people or services as some have in the past. We must treat prophecy as holy.

Getting the Prophetic Unction

This can be difficult for prophetic people to do. Often we don't comprehend the holiness of prophecy. We want to be God's man or woman for the hour, but we don't want to spend the hours in prayer necessary to sustain a consistency of character. Although prophecy may be a gift, it will be effective only when it is infused with energy from the power source of personal and corporate prayer. As such, we must raise the prayer standard before we can raise the prophecy standard amidst God's prophets.

God is calling His prophetic people to their prayer closets once again. Before we can give words from

God, we must receive the anointing of God. As Leonard Ravenhill has said, "With all thy getting get unction." In other words, we need the unction to function in prophetic ministry, hour after hour. If we do not have the unction, then the functionality of our prophetic ministry will be greatly diminished, as will the character of our prophecies.

Prophecy backed by prayer is powerful and productive. Prayer is a wonderful key that will unlock a greater dimension within the prophetic ministry. We need to start turning this key so that we can envision a higher plane. Eagles by nature must fly toward the sun to pursue the heights to which they are called. We cannot see the "big" picture if we are constantly at ground level in our discernment. Nor can we reach the pinnacles of grace without the wings of prayer.

Riding the Wings of Prayer

The eagle's wings are fearfully and wonderfully made, giving it the ability to reach heights that no other creature can. The sky is where it finds freedom. In the same way, we as prophets can find the freedom we crave only in the secret place of prayer. The freedom eludes us because we seek it from men. When we go instead to God in earnest prayer, we will not be denied the freedom He delights in giving to us.

Prophetic people can find true emancipation through the wings of prayer. This frees them to share the prophecies they receive, for they have been endued with power and purpose from on high. This is the high calling of God's prophetic people: to boldly go where God directs them to go through the vehicles of prayer, praise, and prophecy. And the church is longing for them to obey this calling rather than promoting their fleshly agendas.

Serving Through Submission

When prophets become willing to lay down the idols in their hearts, God's people will become willing to follow their example. This means prophets cannot hold onto the idols of pride, rebellion, and insubordination that has held the prophetic ministry in the throes of godly discipline (Heb. 12:7,11). Needless to say, much of the discipline in recent months and years has been well deserved. The need for prophets to be held accountable is crucial to our mission.

How, then, can prophetic people be held accountable? What are the appropriate procedures for holding them accountable? When should discipline be applied? These are the questions that leaders within the church are asking. I believe it is time that we start finding solutions if we are to raise the prophecy standard in the church.

The church needs to know the difference between genuine and false or inaccurate prophecies. We must understand that not all prophecies are the same. Some are good, and some are very bad. Discerning the difference will enable us to hold fast to what is good so that we do not despise prophesying. This is my goal in writing this chapter dealing with the issue of false and inaccurate prophecy.

Making Prophecy Work

Thus far we have laid the foundation of what prophecy is and how it should function in the church. When we build upon this foundation, we will have a better chance of avoiding the problems associated with false and inaccurate prophecy. This will prepare us so that when we encounter false or inaccurate prophecies, we will have the systems in place to handle them so we will not be defeated.

Unfortunately, the church today, for the most part, has not understood how to establish the systems necessary to deal with false or inaccurate prophecies. This has created tension and frustration among leaders within the church. Prophets have become suspect, because pastors and other leaders have not known how to handle false or inaccurate prophecy. As a result, church leaders have come to despise prophetic ministry in some cases.

In many ways, leaders have looked for a scapegoat to blame for the transgressions within prophetic ministry. Prophets are the obvious targets, and in some cases they are to blame. However, I believe that there are larger issues that the church must address before pointing the finger of blame at one ministry group. This is why I ask you to consider what I am writing about raising the standard of prophecy in the church. And this doesn't fall only on prophets, but also on leaders within the body of Christ.

The Leadership Initiative

In truth, we must accept some of the blame for not fully understanding the nature of prophecy or preparing God's people to receive the prophetic word. Prophecy is not a toy; it is an immensely powerful gift designed to prepare the church to fulfill her destiny in Christ. Because of this, false or inaccurate prophecy can do great damage to the soul of the church if it is not dealt with swiftly by its leaders. This means the responsibility for the administration of prophecy falls squarely on our shoulders.

We must accept responsibility for the shoddy way we have allowed prophecy to function within the church and for not covering prophets or God's people in the process. We have hoped that everything would work out, but it often hasn't. We have hidden our heads in the sand, hoping that these things would pass, and they have not. Until we confront our own inadequacy in how we have governed prophecy, we will get what we deserve: fruity prophets and flaky prophecies.

This chapter is a wake-up call to leaders within the church. We cannot ignore the problems associated with false or inaccurate prophecy and still expect to receive the blessings of genuine prophecy. Instead, we must take action to set up the systems that will prevent people from falling away through parking-lot prophecies. As such, we must realize how important these systems or boundaries are in dealing with false or inaccurate prophecy in the lives of God's people.

Eliminating False Prophecy

I believe that one of the primary ways for the effects of false prophecy to be eliminated in the church is to establish some good rules for prophecy. This means we must allow prophecy to function in accordance with God's written word. The Bible is our blueprint for dealing with prophecy. As such, we must find out what God's word says about what to do with false or inaccurate prophecy.

First, what is false prophecy, and how is it distinguished from inaccurate prophecy? A false prophet is someone who speaks under the power of a demon (Deut. 13:1-3). Therefore, false prophecy derives its power from evil spirits. In other words, false prophecy is supernatural in nature and demonic in origin. This is why the Bible so clearly warns us against false prophecy: it is a doorway for the devil to enter our lives. We must be on guard against false prophecy.

By and large, false prophecy doesn't function in the church; it usually functions in the world through psychics, fortunetellers, necromancers, soothsayers, channelers, and so on. Examples of false prophets are Jeanne Dixon, Edgar Cacey, and others, even though what they say sometimes appears accurate. This is why I say that accuracy can never be the only measure of integrity for prophetic ministry.

False Prophecy in the Church

How and when does false prophecy function in the church? False prophecy enters the church when God's people refuse to hear from God. When we turn a deaf ear to the voice of God, we open ourselves up to the demonic. This can sometimes happen in the form of familiar spirits, religious spirits, or other types of demonic entities who come as angels of light to the church (2 Cor. 11:13-15). In fact, many ministers have been tempted by Satan to seek knowledge from sources other than God.

I am constantly amazed at how many times ministers will seek information from anyone but God. We will spend many hours in board meetings and a few minutes in prayer, and then think that we have heard from God. How foolish! We cannot hear the voice of God if we do not spend time with Him. The prophetic ministry is not a substitute for us hearing from God; it is a sign showing us that we have heard from God. Anyone who continues in this kind of atmosphere is a candidate for false prophecy.

I love what one minister said about leaders who do not hear from God: he said they are "dumb idols." This is quite an indictment against leaders who have become unable to hear the voice of God. If the shepherds cannot hear from God, how then can we expect the sheep to be safe from false prophecy (John 10:27)? So then, the best defense against false prophecy in the church is leaders who can hear from God. We, as leaders, must cultivate through our own quite times the ability to hear from God.

False Prophecy vs. Inaccurate Prophecy

Inaccurate prophecy does not contain true information. If someone prophesies a message that does not include correct information, it is usually an inaccurate prophecy rather than a false one. If this happens to us, we should immediately seek the help of spiritual leaders who will be able to counsel us about any erroneous advice in the word given to us.

The major difference, then, between false and inaccurate prophecy is its source. False prophecy is demonic in origin. Inaccurate prophecy is the result of a prophet speaking out of his own heart (Deut. 18:22). Both can be dangerous if acted upon. This is why we should never casually base any major decisions we make on prophecies that we have received, even if they contain accurate information. If we do, then we will reap the fruits of our own misjudgment and error.

Using Prophecy Wisely

As I was browsing the Internet recently, I came across an article written by someone sharing his disappointment with a certain reputable prophet. This prophet predicted that the writer's daughter would marry a man from a particular place. According to this individual, his daughter went to this place, met someone, and then married him, unaware that he was already married. The writer was shocked when he realized this, and blamed the prophet for missing God and messing up his daughter's life.

This example, although extreme, shows the dangers of basing life's decisions entirely on prophecy. We should almost never make major decisions entirely on prophecy, especially marriage. I believe that this person failed his daughter. He abdicated his authority and left his daughter in the hands of a prophet whom he didn't know. I feel sorry for the person who wrote this article, the daughter who married this ungodly man, and the prophet whose reputation has been tarnished by someone else's foolishness.

I wish that the above example were the exception to the rule; however, it is not. The church is filled with believers who have been tarnished and damaged by the words "Thus saith the Lord." As a prophet, this grieves me, not only because in some cases prophets are to blame, but also because God's people can be so ignorant in the way they deal with prophecy. It utterly amazes me to think that someone could take a prophecy, twist it to his own destruction, and then blame the prophet for giving a word (2 Pet. 3:16). How foolish!

This is the danger of prophecy. Although it is designed to be a blessing, it can become a curse if we do not rightly divide the prophetic word. This is where much of the confusion comes. People often do not understand how to interpret the words given to them. Prophets will often assume that their listeners understand the symbolism or the typology of prophetic words, when in reality they usually do not.

For prophecy to be effective, it must be interpreted. We cannot expect the prophetic word to help us if we do not take the time to seek God about it. Prophecy, as I have said before, is not a substitute for hearing from God ourselves. On the contrary, hearing from God is essential once we have received a prophetic word, because we need to find out what to do with it. We must discover what God desires for us to do and when. In other words, prophecy doesn't end our seeking God, but should spur us toward it.

Seeking God Through Prophecy

Seeking God is one of the lost arts of the church. We do not know how to seek Him. We ask God about a problem, and expect Him to immediately fax back a solution. This mentality is foreign to the word of God. God expects those who receive prophetic words to pursue Him for their fulfillment. This is our responsibility once we have received a prophetic word. The scriptures say that through faith and patience they inherited the promises of God

(Heb. 6:12). This is Biblical truth.

We need to start reading our Bible again before we start seeking prophecies. This is one of the problems in the church today: everyone is seeking a word from a prophet without seeking the God of the prophet. We have idols in our hearts that we must lay down. The scriptures declare that if we do not do this, then prophets will answer us according to the idols in our hearts (Ezek. 14:4). I have to wonder if this is a reason why there are so many unfulfilled prophecies in the body of Christ.

Hear me! We need a radical transformation in how we view prophecy. We cannot always blame God's prophets for missing it; we must take responsibility for our own actions. If we want the blessing of prophecy, then we must be willing to pay the price of pursuing God in the secret place of prayer. Don't blame the prophet if you haven't prayed the prophecy. And if you have prayed the prophecy, continue seeking the God of the prophecy, and your life will not be ruined by a false or inaccurate word.

This is an area where many leaders have failed to provide guidance to the church, and this is one of the major reasons why there are so many unfulfilled prophecies. I believe that the majority of unfulfilled prophecies in the body of Christ are really the fault of the hearer of the word rather than the messenger. I am of the opinion that false or inaccurate prophecy makes up a very small percentage of the unfulfilled prophecies in the body of Christ.

Releasing Your Prophecy's Power

I believe there are many untapped prophecies in the body of Christ that are just waiting to happen. We need to reread the prophecies we have been given so that we may understand them in the light of God's word. I am hopeful that this book will provide some guidance as to what to do to see your prophecies fulfilled. Why am I doing this? Because I want God's will to be done in your life. By definition, fulfilled prophecy is the unveiling of His will in our lives.

As we move forward, I will share with you the major reasons prophecies fail. Whether you believe this or not, prophecies can fail. The Bible is full of such instances. In fact, the Bible tells us that these things were written for our example (1 Cor. 10:11). This is the truth that you may not have heard about prophecy. And for some of you, it may be hard to hear. I hope that you will keep an open mind as we go on.

My desire in doing this is not to point the finger of blame, but to release the power of God. I am trusting

God to take the things I have written and to communicate them deep into your spirit. I pray that the enemy would be bound, and that the Spirit of God would be released upon you now. I am asking God to recharge the prophetic words in your life and to endue you with fresh power from on high. When this happens, may God receive all the glory.

I pray God's richest blessings upon you and trust that you will receive the engrafted word that is able to save your soul. The cry of God to the church in this hour is: "Awake, awake, put on thy strength" (Is. 52:1). May God help us to put on the strength of the prophetic words that we have received.

Chapter Three

Handling
Prophecy With
Care

Prophecy and prophetic people are gifts to the church. I think that this truth is often overlooked by many who have suffered through the effects of false or inaccurate prophecy. Yet unless we understand this, we could lose the gift entirely. I have often found that what we do not appreciate can be taken from us. The same is true of those believers who are gifts to the church because of their prophetic abilities.

Hearing from God is probably the single most important thing that we need daily. Without His voice in our lives, we are truly lost and we lose sight of what we should do. We wander aimlessly through life and make very little headway toward our destiny if we do not hear clearly what the Holy Spirit is saying to us individually. This is how important prophecy and prophetic people are to us—we desperately need them.

The Blessing of Genuine Prophecy

The problems in prophecy are minor in comparison to its blessing. When we receive a true prophetic word from God, our lives are radically changed. I have been blessed many times through the prophetic word. These words have become cherished treasures in my life as I pursue the will of God. I am grateful for the people who gave me these words, and for God who spoke through them to me.

There was a time in my life where I was suffering more than I can even convey to you. I literally lost touch with reality. My mind was torn by the spiritual conflict that I experienced as a new believer. For three years, I sought to break free from this oppression, but to no avail—until I received a true

prophetic word. That word broke the bonds of afflic-
tion the enemy had used to bind me. My soul was set
free, and I am here today because of that word.

What would have happened had I not received that
word? I don't even want to think about it. I could have
easily slipped into even greater delusion. I needed the
power of that prophetic word to set me free. We all
need the power resident in the prophetic word to fulfill our destiny. Remember that we have an adversary,
the devil, who is always wandering about seeking
whom he may devour (1 Pet. 5:8). I would have been
devoured had it not been for this prophetic word.

I believe that much of the church is weakened
because the enemy is devouring their members. This
has happened because many pastors and leaders have
prevented them from receiving prophetic ministry.
We all need prophecy, from the least to the greatest
believer. I can say this because all of us need to clearly
hear from God what He wants us to do. And this is
what prophecy brings to the church: a clear voice
from God.

Prophecy—A Compass from God

A clear voice of prophecy can become a compass in
our lives that will lead us on a path toward our destiny in Christ. This is what prophecy is designed to

do for each and every believer who receives it. Prophecy can help us do the will of God even if, at the time, we do not completely understand what the prophetic word is trying to tell us.

We need the voice of prophecy in the church. At the same time, we need to clarify the role of believers in fulfilling prophecy. Many believers think that once they receive a prophecy, they don't have to do anything to see it come to pass. The truth is, once you receive a prophecy, you have more that you are called to do, not less. In other words, every prophecy is a call to action by God.

Two of the primary purposes of prophecy are to disclose who we are called to be, and what we are called to do. These are important reasons for us to receive and regard the prophecies given to us. This is why it is important for us to determine a given source of prophecy. Once we determine a prophecy's source, then we can begin to act upon it to see it come to pass in our lives.

This chapter assumes that the prophecy we receive is accurate and from God. As we saw in the last chapter, this is not always the case. There are times when prophecies may be false or contain inaccurate information. When this happens, we need to prove the prophecy that we have received. We should take it to our spiritual leaders, asking them for their input regarding the prophetic word. This will prevent us from making major mistakes in our lives based upon false or inaccurate words.

Fulfilling Your Prophecies

Assuming that the prophetic word is true, we need to know what to do once we have received a prophecy. This is very often misunderstood within the body of Christ. Few leaders truly know how to prepare their people to act on their prophecies, which is why so many prophecies are unfulfilled. Hence, this chapter will do two things: train believers what to do once they have received a prophecy, and help leaders walk with people toward the path of fulfilled prophecies.

The good news is that God is ready and willing to help us to see our prophecies fulfilled. Heaven is cheering us on as we run with patience the race that is set before us (Heb. 12:1). Therefore, I want to encourage you if you have received a prophecy that hasn't come to pass. Don't give up. Hang on to what God has said, and don't let go. You are about to receive a spiritual boost that will propel you forward into the realms of fulfilled prophecy.

First of all, it is God's will for your prophetic words to come to pass—they are gifts from your Heavenly Father. And as an earthly father will not promise his children something that he cannot do, so also our Heavenly Father will not make promises that He cannot keep (Lk. 11:13). This means that if we have received a word from God, and we hold onto it in faith, we can trust in the sufficiency of God to bring it to pass. Since this is true, we must also know the part that we are to play in seeing prophetic words fulfilled.

Fulfilled prophecy is not just the responsibility of God; it is also our responsibility. If a prophetic word comes from God, it does not necessarily mean that it will come to pass in our lives. This is why we must take great care in understanding the words that we receive. We must know not only what God has spoken to us, but also how we should interpret it. May we never take for granted the words that God gives to us.

This is something I have noticed happening recently in the charismatic/prophetic community. We have taken it for granted that God will always speak to us, which is not a safe assumption. If God withheld His voice for 400 years from a disobedient and gainsaying people, what makes us think that He will not do the same to us? Our lack of appreciation for the prophetic word greatly concerns me, because we may actually be stealing the very thing from our churches that we so desperately need—to hear the voice of God.

Valuing Prophets and Prophecy

Our commitment to the prophetic word must be genuine. We must have a heartfelt desire to hear the voice of God. It is this commitment to the prophetic word that will help us cultivate a generous attitude toward prophetic people. When we see the value that these people bring into our lives, we will do whatever it takes to keep them there. This is the kind of commitment that we, as believers in the prophetic word, must have toward God's anointed vessels of prophecy.

Why am I saying all of this? Because I have found a general distrust and apathy toward prophecy sweeping through the body of Christ, especially among leaders. We have become desensitized to the value of prophecy and prophetic people. We have taken it for granted that prophecy and prophetic people will always be there, but this is not a valid assumption. God may be silent just to allow us to feel the void that a lack of His voice brings (Amos 8:11).

As a prophetic leader within the church, this is one of my greatest concerns. The demands placed on prophetic people are not only unreasonable in many cases, but are unsound in practice. Our desire to pastor the prophetic community has held it in bondage to immaturity. This is one of the main reasons why we have to go outside the local church to hear mature voices of prophecy from the worldwide church. I do not believe this to be a good thing for the church, either local or worldwide.

These are some of the many reasons why I have written this chapter. I am hoping to help believers understand their part in the process of prophecy.

Learning the Prophetic Language

We all have a part to play in seeing prophecy fulfilled. We have seen that God is trustworthy. When He gives us a prophecy, He will stand behind it to see it accomplished in our lives. Because of this, we need to understand that unfulfilled prophecy is mainly due to our lack of correct response, if the prophecy is genuine. We must learn what to do with prophecy and how to handle its difficult terminology.

The prophetic language is like all languages: we must become fluent in it before it can be useful. Many people take courses to learn other languages. They do this to increase the value of their life, possibly in love, career, politics, or in some other way. If this is true in the natural life, what makes us think that it would involve any less work in the spiritual?

The truth is that if we want to hear what God has

to say, we will have to learn His language. This comes more naturally to some than to others, just as certain people are able to more easily interpret spiritual things. This can be a gift from God, or it can be a result of environment. We all tend to communicate in the language of those around us, especially when we learn it as children.

Interpreting What God Is Saying

I believe that the language we use to communicate within the church is often determined by the spiritual leaders who have influenced us. These individuals have shaped our world view as well as the way we communicate. This means that some of us, by virtue of the environment that we grow up in, will have an easier time hearing from God. Why? Because those who nurtured us as we were spiritual newborns imparted the ability to understand and interpret the voice of God.

For others, we may have received this divine ability as a gift from God. He has placed interpreters in the body of Christ (1 Cor. 14:28). These individuals are able to interpret the language in which God speaks. They are extremely important members of the body of Christ, because they help us hear what God is saying through prophecy. And this means that what God says through prophecy may not always be clear to us immediately.

The oldest book in the Bible, the book of Job, describes this saying, "For God speaks once, yea twice, yet man perceiveth it not..." (Job 33:14). We just do not hear what God has to say very often. In other words, we just don't get it. Then God sends someone into our lives to help us. "If there be a messenger, one among a thousand, to show unto man his uprightness: Then He is gracious unto him, and saith, deliver him from going down to the pit" (Job 33:23,24).

Seeking God for Understanding

The quality of our lives is often determined by the words we receive from God through prophecy. I am not saying this to scare you, but to make you aware of the responsibility that we have as the children of God. He holds us accountable for the things we do, or don't do, even if we are ignorant or unaware of them (Rom. 14:12). This can be a frightening thought, but it is reality. Right now the things that are happening in your life reflect whether or not you have heard from God.

In the kingdom of God, there are those who have and those who have not heard from Him. Jesus said, "those who have shall be given more but those who have not even that which they have shall be taken away" (Matt. 13:12). This means that when we hear from God through prophecy, and seek Him for the interpretation, then we will be given more prophecy. If this is true, then wouldn't it make sense that the contrary is true as well?

I hope that you hear what I am saying. We have an awesome opportunity and responsibility set before us when we receive prophecy. Immediately the call upon us is clear: we must seek God for the interpretation of the prophecy we have been given. This means that we are without excuse if we do not see our prophecies fulfilled. We cannot blame the prophet for the unfulfilled words given, if we ourselves have not sought God for the interpretation.

This is a sobering thought, and one that we need to be made aware of. It is not the responsibility of the person prophesying to interpret for us. We ourselves are responsible for understanding the prophecies that have been given to us. God is the one who has given us this responsibility, and it is one that we must take seriously if we want to see the prophecies fulfilled.

Doing What Your Prophecy Says

Yet this is only a first step to seeing prophecy

fulfilled. There are many other things that God has called us to do once we receive a prophecy from Him. Understanding prophecy is vital in our ability to do it, but action gives it power. In other words, understanding the prophecies gives us the ability to do what God wants us to do, and it is in the actual doing of God's will that we see a release of His power on our behalf.

This is where so many people fall short of seeing their prophecies fulfilled: they never do what God is asking them to do through the prophecy. Either they don't understand, they have not taken the initiative, or they are unwilling to do what they need to do. These are the three main things that prevent most people from seeing their prophecies fulfilled, and they all fall into the category of unbelief.

Why do I call this unbelief? Because whether we don't understand what God wants us to do, or we do understand and are not doing it, we are accountable for what God has spoken to us. In other words, God has placed faith in our hearts, and we just haven't taken the time to act upon it. Remember faith comes by hearing and hearing by the word of God (Rom. 10:17). Once we have heard, we are in a position to obey. And our obedience to what God has said is faith that works.

Having Faith in Your Prophecy

This was one of the main reasons, according to scripture, that God was constantly irritated with the children of Israel. They heard what He said, but they didn't do what He told them to do. According to the writer of Hebrews, "The word preached did not profit them, not being mixed with faith in them that heard it" (Heb. 4:2). In other words, doing what God tells us to do in prophecy is what enables us to see it fulfilled in our lives—this is faith.

This faith is a gift from God that comes through hearing and obeying what He has said. I will not discuss what real faith is in this book, but I want you to know that I have been writing an extremely important book on faith for the past 10 years, and look forward to seeing it released in the near future. In that book, I detail what Biblical faith is and what it is not.

Suffice it to say that real faith is a vital element in seeing our prophecies fulfilled. In other words, doing what God has said is a fundamental rule, and unless we obey, we will not see prophecies come true in our lives. Because of this, we must not only seek to understand what God has said to us through prophecy, we must determine if He has given any action commands through it.

Explicit and Implied Actions in Prophecy

This is not always as easy as it sounds. Often what God says to us through prophecy is veiled. Occasionally the action commands He gives to us are clear, but this is not always the case. Sometimes God will not tell us to do anything in the prophecy itself, but an action is implied by what He is speaking to us. It is these implied actions that can make the difference in seeing our prophecies entirely fulfilled.

To help you understand what I am saying, I will use some prophecies that I have received from various individuals to illustrate. One of the prophecies I received came from John Paul Jackson, a reputable prophet I became acquainted with in 1996. The Lord allowed me to spend some time with him when I went to the Dallas/Ft. Worth area in 1998. We had lunch a couple of times and discussed several things.

The prophecy that John Paul gave me said, "God has given you a real gift, a specialized revelatory gift … especially in the area of government and administration. The Lord will open up a whole panoramic view for you … according to 1 Cor. 2." This prophecy is from a reputable prophet; it is a genuine word from God. I have greatly reduced the overall content in the word because I want to convey a point to you. I want to show you several action commands that are implied but are not said.

When the Lord said through John Paul that I have "a real gift," the implication was that I would be working with some people who don't have such gifts. He also said I would be using the gift in the "areas of government and administration," so I will have to learn how to deal with people diplomatically as an ambassador for Christ. Additionally, he said that I would see "a whole panoramic view according to 1 Cor. 2." This means I will see what others do not. I will need to learn how to communicate on their level.

None of these things were in the original prophecy by John Paul, and yet they are implied by what was spoken. This is what will often happen in prophecy. God will speak to us, and within His words there will be implied commands. The commands are in the prophecy by John Paul, although they are not stated, and it is important for me to obey them to see the prophecy fulfilled.

Another example of a prophecy with implied commands is one given to me by a prophet named Rick Calhoun in 1992. In this prophecy several commands were given, both explicit and implied. The prophecy stated, "My son, I have called you as my prophet. I have called you to be a clarion in this day and this hour. I will raise you up, even thrust you out, to speak my word to the nations. I am blessing you, my son. I am leading you into the deeper things of God. I am putting a hunger in your heart..."

Although this prophecy appears to have no overt commands whatsoever, in reality God is clearly saying what He expects of me. The general sense of this word is that I was not ready, so I must not go out yet. This command is revealed through what was implied in the prophecy. What action did God want me to take? He wanted me to wait for Him, and to bring me forth as His prophet in the right timeframe.

So then, not everything given in prophecy is always explicitly stated, but will often be implied. Therefore, we need to listen what God is really saying to us, whether it is explicit or implicit. This is very important. If I didn't do what God said and did not wait for Him to bring me forth at the right time, I might have failed in the things that God wanted to do.

What did God do during this time of waiting? One of the most important things was that He healed me. I had been hurt very deeply by several individuals. People I had trusted took advantage of me, and wounded me as a result. In some cases, the harm appeared to be unintentional, but in others the attacks were blatant. If I had allowed this to continue, I would have been greatly affected in my ability to help people through prophecy. I might have even communicated this through the prophecies I gave.

Receiving Prophecy With a Good Heart

Because prophecy is communicated from one heart to another, as a prophet I must guard my own heart against anything unclean being able to enter and to contaminate what I am saying. This can be very difficult, for we live in a world saturated with sin. Unless I make a concerted effort to prevent sin from entering my heart, I might communicate an unhealthy attitude to those I am speaking to prophetically. This is how important it is for me to maintain the clear waters of a pure heart in ministry (Prov. 4:23).

In the same way, when you receive a prophecy, the way you receive it can have a direct impact upon its fulfillment. We can prevent prophecies from coming to pass in our lives through wrong heart attitudes and motives. This goes even deeper than not doing what a prophecy says. It also speaks to becoming the person God wants us to be. In other words, for prophecies to be fulfilled in our lives, we must not only do them, but must become them.

This is the ultimate goal of prophecy. We must not only change what happens in our lives, but also who we are as individuals. God desires to get to the heart of the matter when He speaks to us prophetically. He is looking to make us into the men and women that He wants us to be. Because of this, prophecy must be allowed to change the way we think and how we do things. Our character must change and conform to that revealed in the prophetic word.

This is the second main reason prophecies fail, and it is what we will discuss in the next chapter as we press forward to seeing our prophecies fulfilled.

Chapter Four

The Road to Fulfilled Prophecy

The road to fulfilled prophecy is not an easy one. It is wrought with many pitfalls, both for the one who is giving and the one who is receiving prophecy. Prophecy is not an exact science. We cannot always expect one hundred percent accuracy. This is where the whole realm of grace comes into play in prophecy. We need to give one another the grace that each of us needs to grow.

Greasing the Wheels of Prophecy
With Grace

Grace is needed in giving prophecy. It is not easy to tell someone the intimate details of their life. This is especially true with an individual who has built up an image within the church. Prophecy doesn't always confirm a person's own opinion about himself, so it can be difficult for him to accept prophetic words that contradict that opinion. This will often open the one prophesying to unexpected hostility.

At the same time, the one receiving prophecy needs grace. The prophetic word isn't always as clear as we hope it would be. Prophets see in part and prophesy in part (1 Cor. 13:9). Because of this, it can be very very difficult to put the pieces of prophecy together to come up with a picture of what should be done. This is why we need grace both from the person prophesying and the spiritual leaders in our lives to help us work out the important details.

So then, prophecy needs plenty of grace, and all those involved in prophecy need to have humble hearts (1 Pet. 5:5,6). Those who humble themselves in the sight of the Lord will be lifted up. Prophecy requires humility. Without this vital aspect of Christ's character in our lives, we will not have the grace necessary to walk in the realm of prophecy. The doorway to the realm of prophecy is grace, and humility paves the way for grace to be active in our lives.

All of us who speak prophetically need to be willing to admit our mistakes in prophesying. Admitting such mistakes doesn't take away from the prophetic call or anointing upon our lives. In fact, it enables us to more fully walk in the grace of the prophetic call that God has given to us. And it makes us less susceptible to the "need to be right."

Problems in Prophecy

Dogma can be a real hindrance to us fulfilling our calling in God. This is why we need to guard against the attitude of always being right. None of us is always right all the time. Even the most mature prophets will occasionally miss it, either in the word itself or in the interpretation of a word. This is not uncommon, and it is one reason why we are called not to "despise not prophesyings;" but to "prove all things; holding fast that which is good" (1 Thes. 5:20,21).

If the church lived by this principle that Paul wrote about prophecy, we would not have the problems we have today. This simple rule would prevent a lot of the foolish things people say or do in the name of God. Additionally, if we were to handle prophecy according to the scripture, we would not have the problems that come as a result of foolish and ignorant men. All prophecies must be judged by other prophets, and we must make room for prophets to allow this to happen in the church.

Moreover, if we want prophecy to take effect in our lives, we must be willing to receive prophecy with humility. We cannot go to God with idols in our hearts and expect to hear from Him clearly. In fact, I think that many of the people receiving prophecy in conferences sponsored by various prophetic ministries have idols in their hearts. The major problem is that we have no clear requirements for those receiving prophetic ministry.

Giving and Receiving Good Prophecy

I believe this must change. We need to examine the present trend of allowing people to receive prophetic ministry just because they attend our conferences. There must be an increase in the overall accountability of those prophesying and those receiving prophecy. We cannot have one without the other, as some have proposed. If we place stringent requirements on those prophesying, we should place the same requirements on those receiving prophetic ministry.

The church needs a basic understanding of the

value of the prophetic word and how to preserve its integrity. We must guard against foolish prophecies that beget questions rather than edify the body. Also, we must guard against folly in the hearts of those receiving prophetic ministry. There must be an over-all balance of giving and receiving the prophetic word. And we must come to the place that everyone is edified by the prophetic word, which is not happening today (1 Cor. 14:26).

I have said all this because character is an important component of prophecy, both in giving and receiving. When we understand that our character magnifies the prophet's effectiveness and the prophecy's power, most of us will bend over backward to walk in Christlike character. This is the bottom line of prophetic ministry: it encourages us to live our lives like Christ.

How Prophecy Has Changed My Life

Our character is extremely important in the fulfill-ment of the prophetic words that we receive. In fact, the prophetic word is very often spoken to show us certain aspects of our lives that God would like us to change. We should always view the prophetic word as a tool for developing our character in God. As such, all prophetic words will challenge us as we receive, believe, and walk in them.

Living prophetically means that we are willing to allow the master potter to mold us into the vessels He wants us to be. This quality of openness is what prepares our hearts to receive the prophetic word. It is the seed-bed that will cause the prophetic word to take root and grow effectively in our lives. This is why I want to encourage you to receive prophecy, not to confirm what you want to hear, but to hear what God has to say. These can often be two very different things.

I have found through my own experience that rarely does a person prophesying speak to the exact need that I have at a particular time. Often the words spoken have been quite different from what I needed. I once required guidance from God about my finances when a prophetic conference happened to be going on in my area. So I went, expecting to hear from God about my finances.

This is the word that I received: "My Son, I have called you to be my prophet. I have called you to be a clarion in this day and this hour. I will raise you up, even thrust you out, to speak my words to the nation...." Today this word is a real comfort to me regarding the call of God upon my life, but back when it was given, I was perplexed as to why God did not speak to me about my finances. In fact, the week after this word was given, I was evicted from my apartment and found myself homeless.

This was not a fun experience, but it is a wonderful illustration about how God can speak to us concerning things that are different from what we want or think we should hear. Does this mean that God is not concerned about our need if He doesn't speak about it in prophecy? The answer is no. God is always concerned about our needs. He understands that we are made of flesh and blood and need to be fed, housed, and clothed. He knows our every need.

Then why does God often not speak to our points of immediate need in prophecy? Because He wants to help us get our eyes off our need and onto Him, for he is able to meet our need. God met my need for housing after I was homeless for a week. The place that He provided was ideal for me at the time. The expense was just right, and it had a great view in a great neighborhood. It was there that I finished the writing of my first book, *Decade of Destiny*.

God Really Does Know What He Is Doing

What I want you to understand is that prophecy doesn't replace the Word of God or our need to have faith in God's word. It is designed to speak to us about what He wants us to know that will help us in the present or future. This means that prophecy is forward looking. Even when a prophecy touches upon an area of our past, it is designed to help us in the present or future areas of our lives. God will never bring up things from the past that He doesn't intend to heal.

We need to understand that God is much wiser than we are. I think we mentally assent to understanding and believing this, but when it comes right down to it, we think that we know what is best. This is why so many people today have a difficult time trusting God. We cannot trust Him because we don't really think that He knows everything. We believe that if we can get a grasp on things, we can "help God out." Isn't this foolish?

There have even been some teachings that have made our part more than it really is. Some have called this the "manifest sons of God" teaching. Many teachings are based upon similar principles. The basic theology is that it is up to us. If we don't do it, it won't get done. The pressure is on us. God has done everything He can for us. All these things add up to the same flawed philosophy that rules out God's sovereignty.

Prophecy should help us understand the responsibility of man and the sovereignty of God. Both are vital as we seek to fulfill prophecy. We cannot expect our faith mindset to rule out the word of prophecy that comes our way. Additionally, we cannot expect God to respond to us in an evangelical fashion just because we were raised in evangelical churches. This means we cannot, and should not, rule out prophecies that appear intellectually unsound.

Receiving Prophecy Even When It Doesn't Make Sense

God is sovereign, and when He speaks to us through prophecy, He will do so from His sovereign perspective, not our earthly one. John the Baptist said, "He that is of the earth is earthly and speaketh of the earth…" (John 3:31). Yet about Jesus he says, "He that cometh from heaven is above all. And what he hath seen and heard He testifieth; and no man receiveth His testimony. He that hath received His testimony hath set to his seal that God is true" (John 3:31-33).

John the Baptist's words express awesome realities that we must understand when we consider prophecy. Prophecy is not the will of man; it is the word of God being conveyed through a human vessel. Yet even though the message is conveyed through a fallible instrument, it doesn't mean that the words are not of God. Furthermore, Jesus was speaking under the influence of God's Spirit of prophecy. This is why the scriptures say, "For He whom God hath sent speaketh the words of God…" (John 3:34).

The living word of God, Jesus Christ, spoke the rhema word of God under the unction of the spirit of prophecy throughout His entire ministry. What an example that Jesus has set for us. No wonder the lives of those to whom He spoke were forever changed—He was prophesying His character through His words. This is what drew people to Jesus, and it is also what pushed many away. And if we speak the prophetic word, we can expect no less from those around us today.

Being Goaded by God

I hope you hear what I am saying: Real prophecy changes lives forever. Something radical happens to us when we hear the real word of God. It provokes a response from us. We respond to prophecy in some way—either by ignoring it, rationalizing it, refusing it, or receiving it and seeing it fulfilled in our lives. These are the choices set before us once we receive a prophetic word from God, no matter who we are or our position in life. Genuine prophecy evokes a response from us (Lk. 4:18-29).

Why do we need to know this? Because how we respond to prophecy has a great impact on whether it is fulfilled in our lives or is repelled like water off a duck's back. If we respond one way, we can be changed and conformed into the image of Christ; if another way, we will eventually dry up and burn out. This is one reason why I believe God chose to convey the power of prophecy to Ezekiel in a valley of dry bones—Ezekiel was called to prophesy to dry burned-out individuals (Ezek. 37).

Being burned out doesn't have to cause us to drop out of the race. God can restore us to a living state if we allow Him to speak into our lives. When God speaks to us, good changes will enter into our lives if we receive what He says. This means we need to be open and receptive to the word of God, spoken through the vehicle of prophecy. If we are, then God can change our lives and conform us to the image of Christ, no matter where we are now.

Some have called this redemptive prophecy. I believe that all prophecy from God is redemptive in nature. In other words, prophecy can redeem us from desperate situations and cause dew to appear upon the desert of our lives to water our hopes, dreams, and aspirations. This is what prophecy should do in you.

It should create hope, faith, and—most importantly—love. God's love should be shed abroad in your heart through the prophetic word.

Prophecy May Test Us

Yet sometimes prophecy may not change our internal heart attitudes but our external circumstances. These changes will be either for our short-term or long-term good. Sometimes prophecy can create an atmosphere for our lives to be tested for a short time, but designed to yield long-term fruit. In this case, the prophetic word will become the vehicle through which God tests our hearts to see if we are ready to receive the promise that He has given to us.

Joseph is an excellent example of this principle in prophecy (Gen. 37). One night while he was sleeping, he received a dream about his calling as a leader. The next day, he shared this dream with his brothers— who just about stoned him for what he said. In fact, they conspire to kill him, but then decide to sell him into slavery. So Joseph had been sitting on top of the world after receiving this great prophetic word about his leadership ability, but the next day he was sold into slavery by his own brothers. This was not exactly what Joseph expected when he received the word of prophecy.

While in Egypt, he served a man named Potipher, and God prospered him. Then Potipher's wife conspired to sleep with Joseph. I imagine she was drooling just thinking about how she was going to entrap him. The only problem was that Joseph didn't fall for the bait. Furiously, she told her husband that Joseph tried to rape her. Joseph was cast into prison. Surprisingly, he wasn't executed.

I can imagine Joseph sitting in that dark and dreary dungeon, just thinking about where he missed God. What could he have done differently? How would he ever get out of this situation? It seemed that the deck was stacked against Joseph—he just couldn't seem to get a break. The word of God says about Joseph's time of trial, "Until the time that his word came, the word of the Lord tried him" (Ps. 105:19). This is a sobering thought about prophecy, isn't it? It's the word of prophecy trying us on for size.

Suffering Through Prophecy

I like to think of it this way. The word of prophecy comes into our lives, and when it comes, it usually doesn't fit. So the prophetic word begins to work specifically on our character. We go through intensive character redevelopment training. This is often associated with trials, temptations, sufferings, and afflictions (1 Pet. 1:6,7). All of these begin to work on our character, molding and shaping us to the word of prophecy that we have received.

Maybe you, like Joseph, have received a prophecy about a great thing that would happen in your life someday, but the next day all hell broke loose. Suddenly your business went bankrupt, your marriage went sour, your friends deserted or betrayed you, or your church abandoned you. You were brought to the end of your rope. When all hope was lost, it was then that God began to work in your life. You were brought into the process of what a friend of mine calls "holy frustration."

When this happens, it is easy to look for someone or something to blame. We look everywhere for the solution to our problem. In fact, some of us come to the place where we give up and lose heart because things got tougher than we expected. We can't hold on to what we have been given by God, because we have lost the grip on our lives. We find that once our control is gone, so is our faith in God. This can be the hardest point any person will ever come to in life.

One prophet has called this experience the dark night of the soul. This is when we come to the place where we can no longer remain as we were before the word came. Instead, we become broken and submissive to Christ: glady giving up what we have so we can receive what He has. I like to think of it this way. It is as if we have been in a desert for many days without water. We have given up all hope of finding refreshment. This is the dark night of the soul.

Thankfully, when a prophecy is real, God does not leave us in this dark night forever. He will set before us an oasis at just the right time if we remain true to pursue Him. It is in our pursuit of God that we become more like Him. We begin to see Him more clearly. Our eyes become opened and our hearts are filled with life. We have changed. We have crossed a bridge for which there is no passage back. We have entered into the prophetic word.

Fully Entering Your Prophecy

This entry into the prophetic word is just the beginning of our journey toward its fulfillment. If we stay on track in the character that has been formed in us, we will receive the prize. However, if we choose to change back to our old selves, the word will react by fighting against us. We will find ourselves spinning our wheels and going nowhere fast. We will be denied the fulfillment of the prophetic word.

Moses is an excellent example of someone who did not completely enter into the fulfillment of the prophecy given to him (Ps. 106:32,33). Moses had a problem with anger. In his youth he had killed a man over a dispute. To deal with Moses' anger problem and other issues, God took him to the desert for 40 years. Talk about heavy-duty dealings. Moses went through the wringer, and yet when push came to shove, he still had a problem with anger, and this prevented his prophecy from being fulfilled.

God Himself gave the prophecy to Moses, so it must have been a genuine word. Yet Moses was not allowed to enter the promised land on this side of life. The prophecy Moses received from the very mouth of God did not come to pass, because Moses failed the prophecy. His character, even though it had substantially changed, had not come to the place for him to receive the promise given to him. This is why he only saw the promised land, but never entered into it.

This is a sobering thought. Moses was the only prophet, besides Jesus, to talk to God face to face. Moses saw God. Some of us think we see God, but Moses actually did. Moses had a burning bush experience. An angel went before him. God spoke to him audibly. We are talking the real deal here. This was a man who intimately knew God. Yet Moses failed to see his prophecy fulfilled because his character never changed as much as God wanted it to.

Joseph, on the other hand, saw his prophecy fulfilled. He was willing to let God deal with him so he could change sufficiently and fully receive what God had promised him. The word of the Lord tried him on for size, and he fit perfectly. This is what God intends for us when we receive a prophetic word—the word of the Lord should change us sufficiently so that it fits us perfectly.

This is the key ingredient missing in much of the church in relation to fulfilled prophecy. Prophecies often fail us because we have failed the prophecies. In other words, our character is not sufficient for us to handle the word that the Lord has given to us. As a result, we can spend years waiting for the fulfillment of a prophecy that is waiting on us to change.

I believe that this chapter can forever change your perspective of prophecy. Now that you have the truth about fulfilled and unfulfilled prophecy, you are a real threat to the devil. The devil hates it when God's people start seeing their prophecies fulfilled. Remember that prophecy is the will of God for your life, and it is also a sword in the hand of God to drive back the forces of darkness that hold this world in bondage.

You can be a bondage breaker in the lives of many people as you pursue the fulfillment of the prophecies given to you. As such, I pray that the God would fill you with His glory to such a degree that your life is transformed into the likeness of Jesus Christ, His Son, against whom no devil may stand.

A Final Thought

I hope you have enjoyed learning some of the principles of the prophetic that I have taught in this chapter. Although there are many wonderful books about the prophetic, few have touched on unfulfilled prophecy. As a result, many people have become confused and disillusioned about their prophecies. Because of this, I wanted to present a practical approach for you to see your prophecies fulfilled.

Fulfilled prophecies produce fulfilled believers. Whenever believers don't see their prophecies being fulfilled, they move into the realm of discontentment. Discontentment becomes prevalent in the Body of Christ when we do not see God moving on our behalf. The problem is that we have been waiting on God to fulfill His promises, and He has been waiting for us to walk in His covenant. Being prophetic means being a person of covenant.

Every believer has a covenant with God, and it is the basis for the prophetic words we receive. We are responsible to walk in that covenant, and when we do, we are enabled to fulfill the will of God that is revealed through prophecy. All true prophecies reveal the specific will of God for our lives and are based upon the covenant that we have with God.

Because of this, we all have responsibilities before God for the prophetic words that we receive. When we hear a prophecy and obey it, we will be given more prophecy that will help us to hear more clearly and serve Him more effectively. We will draw closer to the center of God's will for our lives, and move closer to the person of Jesus. So then, prophecy is designed to align us with God so that we can live our lives for Him on the basis of His covenant, and draw nearer to Him in fellowship.

No wonder God loves prophecy. It helps those who listen and obey, and it draws us near to Him. If the church would learn to love and covet prophecy as the scriptures tell us to, we would begin to see radical changes in the house of God. We would see many people saved, healed, and delivered by the power of God. Believers would be healthier, happier, and holier. This is a good reason for us to have prophecy.

A few inaccurate words and a few false prophets must not be allowed to steal this precious gift from God to the church. The truth is, we need more prophecy in our day, not less. The world is spinning dangerously out of control into hell, and many believers are being plunged into its hellish lifestyle. We cannot hope that this stuff goes away, because it will not. We must be prepared to live in a chaotic world through the vehicle of prophecy.

We are living in the last days, and we need the powerful weapon of prophecy in our arsenal against the devil's devices. We cannot stick our heads in the sand and hope that the enemy leaves us alone, for he will not. Remember what Peter the apostle said, "Be sober, be vigilant; because your adversary the devil, as a roaring lion, walketh about, seeking whom he may devour…" (1 Peter 5:8). This means we will need supernatural information to deal with our supernatural foe.

It is time for the church to realize that she is in a war against a foe who will not give up. The only way to cause the devil to give up is to fight against him. We can truly fight a strategic battle against the enemy with the weapons of our warfare, which are not carnal but mighty through God. One of these weapons is prophecy. I like to imagine prophecy as the main weapon that an everyday believer has against the devil.

If Paul were to write his spiritual warfare sermon to the Ephesian church today, he would probably say something like this, "…and take the gun of the Spirit, which is the prophetic word of God." This is what the church needs to do today: we need to pick up the gun of the Spirit or the prophetic word of God every day. We cannot, yea must not, send believers out into battle unarmed against the devices of the devil. We must give the church the weapons she needs to fight against the powers of darkness.

It is time for the church as a whole to wake up. We have been lulled into sleep by a false sense of security. Our heavenly mindset must become a battle-ready church mindset. We are not in heaven yet, and unless some real changes take place, many of us will end up there without completing the will of God for our lives. This is not what God wants, and it certainly isn't what I want. I want to stand before Jesus and hear Him say, "Well done, good and faithful servant." How about you?

What earthly soldier would go into battle without a gun? No matter how well a soldier is trained to stand and fight without a gun, he is going to run when the enemy comes with his spiritual weapons against him. Maybe this is a reason why so many believers are running from the devil today—we don't have our spiritual guns to fight him with the prophetic word. It is that simple. And we in leadership are going to be held accountable for the way we have prepared our people to live for Christ through the vehicle of prophecy.

I want you to understand what I am saying. If you are a leader or pastor of a church, and do not prepare your people to walk prophetically, you are sending them into battle unarmed. They can know the teachings of the scriptures, understand who they are in Christ, be at peace with all men, walk the faith walk, talk the faith talk, and spend hours in prayer. Yet they can still live defeated lives because they do not have the spiritual gun of prophecy with which to fight.

This is how important prophecy is, and it is why we need more teaching on it. We need practical teaching about how we, as everyday believers, can live prophetic lives. We need to understand the types of prophecy, the purpose of prophecy, the language of prophecy, and more. We cannot settle into stagnation, thinking that we know what prophecy is. In truth, we have barely scratched the surface of what prophecy can and should do in the church and world.

Because of this, by the grace of God, I will be writing another book on *Plugging Into The Spirit of Prophecy*. In that book, I will be writing some things about prophecy you may never have heard. I will be teaching about how different prophecies are designed to do different things in our lives. There are several types of prophecies, and several ways in which prophetic words can come. We need to be open to all of the ways of God through which He wants to speak to us prophetically.

Finally, this is not an end-all, be-all book. I have written about the major reasons that a large portion of Christ's church is kept from seeing prophecies fulfilled. I have done this because I long to see the bride of Christ made ready for her husband through the word of prophecy. I believe that this book will help many people who have been walking outside the blessing and will of God to enter into His will through the vehicle of fulfilled prophecy. To this end is it written.

Contact
Information

To contact Pastor Scott Wallis for speaking engagements,
or other ministry materials, please write or call him at:

All Nation's Worship Center
1100 Larkin Ave., NW Suite
Elgin, IL. 60123

Phone: 847.468.8139
Email: allnationsworship@prodigy.net

CPSIA information can be obtained at www.ICGtesting.com
Printed in the USA
LVOW040700021212

309625LV00001B/17/A